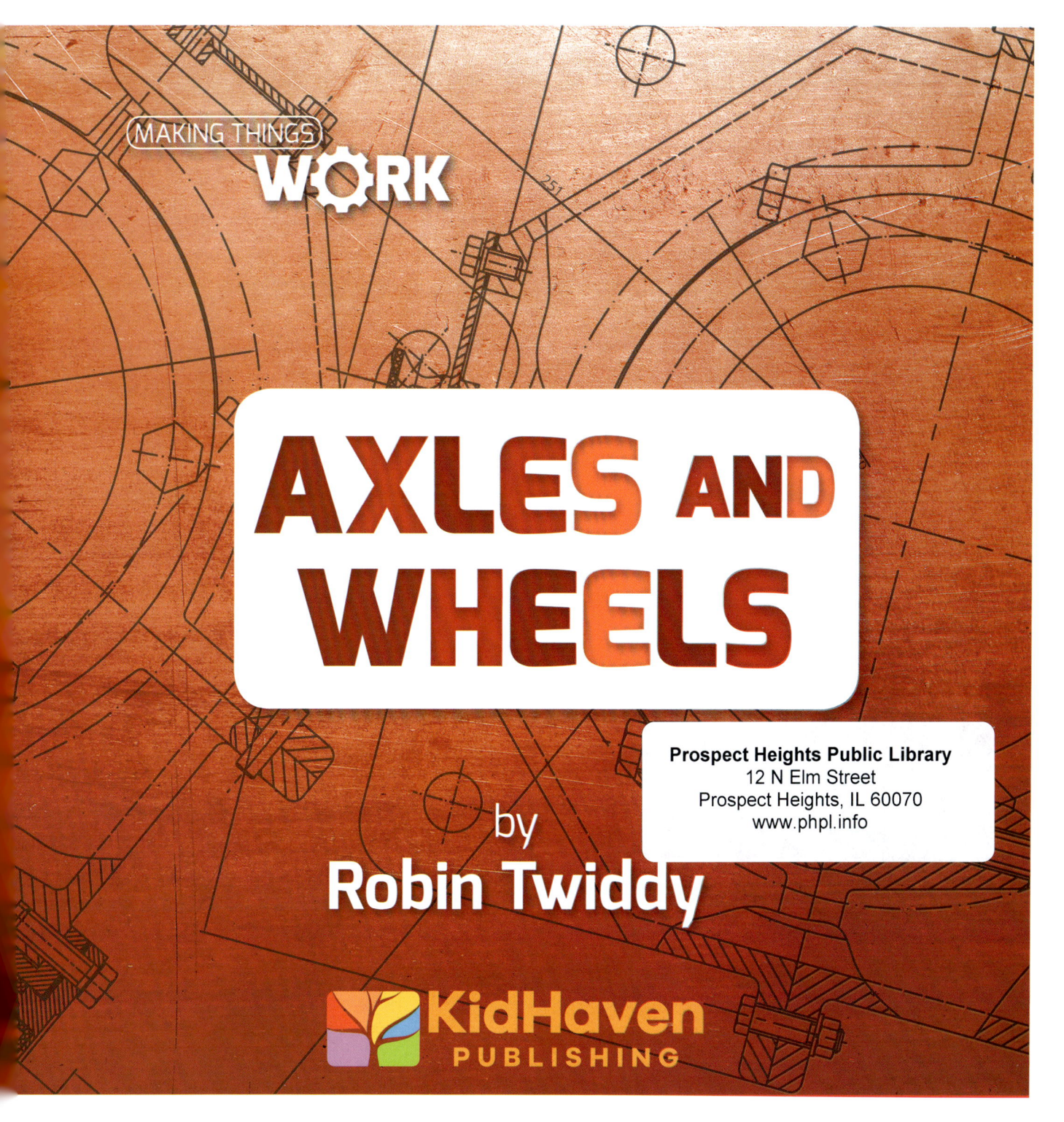

MAKING THINGS WORK

AXLES AND WHEELS

by
Robin Twiddy

Prospect Heights Public Library
12 N Elm Street
Prospect Heights, IL 60070
www.phpl.info

KidHaven
PUBLISHING

Published in 2019 by KidHaven Publishing, an Imprint of Greenhaven Publishing, LLC
353 3rd Avenue, Suite 255, New York, NY 10010

© 2019 Booklife Publishing

This edition is published by arrangement with Booklife Publishing.

All rights reserved. No part of this book may be reproduced in any
form without permission in writing from the publisher, except by a reviewer.

Written by: Robin Twiddy
Edited by: Kristy Holmes
Designed by: Gareth Liddington

Cataloging-in-Publication Data

Names: Twiddy, Robin.
Title: Axles and wheels / Robin Twiddy.
Description: New York : KidHaven Publishing, 2019. | Series: Making things work | Includes glossary and index.
Identifiers: ISBN 9781534529397 (pbk.) | ISBN 9781534529410 (library bound) | ISBN 9781534529403 (6 pack) | ISBN 9781534529427 (ebook)
Subjects: LCSH: Axles--Juvenile literature. | Wheels--Juvenile literature.
Classification: LCC TJ181.5 T963 2019 | DDC 621.8--dc23

Printed in the United States of America

CPSIA compliance information: Batch #BW19KL: For further information contact Greenhaven Publishing LLC, New York, New York at 1-844-317-7404.

Photocredits: Abbreviations: l-left, r-right, b-bottom, t-top, c-centre, m-middle. All images are courtesy of Shutterstock.com.
Cover – Aleksandr Semenov, steamroller_blues, Tatiana Belova, Statson4ik, irra_irra, Pashkovska Tetyana, Whitevector, alextan8, loraks, MiloVad, R-O-M-A, 2 - DeReGe, 4 - Monkey Business Images, 5 - Tatyana Vyc, 6 - MG photos, taboga, Dmitry Kolmakov, Aleksandr Simonov, 7 - tatui suwat, 8 - Jose Elias da Silva Neto, Rudy Balasko, 9 - Monkey Business Images, 10 - noppasit TH, 11 - chonlasub woravichan, 12 - Lopolo, Pla2na, 13 - Pressmaster, 14 - symbiot, 15 - Tatyana Vyc, 16 - wavebreakmedia, 17 - Lisa James, 18 - a_v_d, Poldarkk, Dudarev Mikhail, AG-PHOTOS, 19 - robert cicchetti, 20 - lukethelake, 21 - andy0man, 22 - Monkey Business Images, 23 - Elena Yakusheva, 24 - Ljupco Smokovski.

Images are courtesy of Shutterstock.com. With thanks to Getty Images, Thinkstock Photo and iStockphoto.

All facts, statistics, web addresses and URLs in this book were verified as valid and accurate at time of writing.
No responsibility for any changes to external websites or references can be accepted by either the author or publisher.

CONTENTS

Page 4	Wheels
Page 6	How Wheels Work
Page 8	Axles
Page 10	How Axles Work
Page 12	Fun with Wheels
Page 14	Wheels Come in Different Sizes
Page 16	Helpful Wheels
Page 18	Unexpected Wheels
Page 20	Cogs and Gears
Page 22	Bikes, Wheels, and Axles
Page 24	Glossary and Index

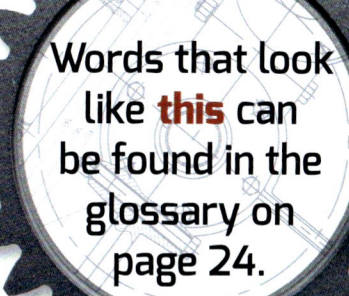

Words that look like *this* can be found in the glossary on page 24.

WHEELS

Wheels are very important. They can help us get from one place to another, like going to school in the car.

Wheels can also be lots of fun. Without wheels, you wouldn't be able to ride your bike or play on a skateboard.

Wheels can be made of many different materials.

HOW WHEELS WORK

There are different types of wheels that come in different sizes. They have different uses.

All wheels are round.

An axle, which runs through the middle of a wheel, allows the wheel to turn and spin.

AXLES

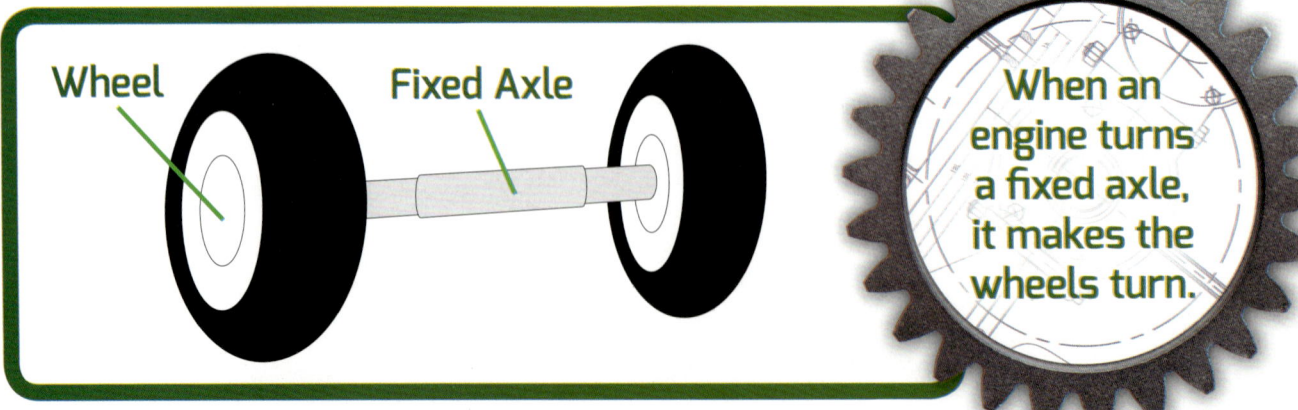

Wheel   Fixed Axle

When an engine turns a fixed axle, it makes the wheels turn.

There are lots of different types of axles. Some axles are fixed to the wheel and turn with the wheel.

Free axles are not fixed to the wheel. These axles will be fixed to something else, such as your bike frame.

Free axles stay still, and the wheels can spin around them.

HOW AXLES WORK

The free axle in your bike has tiny metal balls in it called bearings. These bearings help the wheel turn on the axle without rubbing.

Ball bearings can be very small.

Bearings on an axle are often covered with oil or grease. This helps protect the bearings and makes turning the wheel smoother.

FUN WITH WHEELS

The turbine uses a fixed axle to turn wind into energy.

What do this fidget spinner and this **wind turbine** have in common? They both spin on an axle.

Most things that spin have an axle. This playground merry-go-round is a big wheel on a big axle.

This axle is fixed to the ground.

WHEELS COME IN DIFFERENT SIZES

Some wheels are very big. This tractor needs big wheels to help it drive over rough ground. The big, heavy **tires** make getting through mud easy.

Big Wheels

Small Wheels

The wheels on these rollerblades are small. They are made to roll on smooth ground and do not need to be big like the tractor's wheels.

HELPFUL WHEELS

Some wheelchairs use electric motors to move.

Wheels can help people who cannot walk to get around. This wheelchair moves on its wheels when the user pushes forward.

This wheelbarrow helps move heavy things around, thanks to its helpful wheel and axle.

Some wheelbarrows have two wheels.

UNEXPECTED WHEELS

Wheels are everywhere. We don't always notice them. Sometimes we find wheels in unexpected places.

Steering Wheel

Pulley Wheel

Computer Mouse

Ferris Wheel

This water wheel is turned by the river. It has a fixed axle. Wheels like this were used to grind flour from corn and wheat.

COGS AND GEARS

Teeth

Some machines have cogs and gears inside that make them work. These are wheels that have teeth around them.

When two cogs are lined up together, turning one cog will turn the other.

Cogs with **Interlocking** Teeth

BIKES, WHEELS, AND AXLES

Most bikes have two wheels, but some bikes have more. If you are learning to ride a bike, you might have some extra wheels that help you to **balance**.

This bike has training wheels to help it balance.

Unicycle

Bikes with more wheels are more stable and easier to balance. This unicycle has only one wheel and axle and is very hard to ride.

GLOSSARY

balance — the ability to stay upright
interlocking — locking or fitting together
pulley — a machine that uses ropes and a wheel to lift heavy loads
tires — thick pieces of rubber that go around a wheel
wind turbine — a machine that uses energy from the wind to make electricity

INDEX

bearings 10-11
bikes 5, 9-10, 22-23
cars 4
fidget spinner 12
spinning 7, 9, 12-13
water wheel 19

Prospect Heights Public Library
12 N. Elm Street
Prospect Heights, IL 60070
www.phpl.info